GROUNDCOVER
SERIES

For, and because of, Mo

Acknowledgements

I would like to thank the many people who have contributed
so much towards the making of this book. In particular, I wish
to single out my mother and Bob Drumgold, without whose
support and encouragement the project would certainly not have
reached fruition. Special thanks also go to His Grace the
Duke of Marlborough and Paul Duffie at Blenheim Palace;
the Right Reverend Father Francis Baird at Prinknash Abbey;
the ever-helpful staff of Gloucester Library; Stephen Dunn;
Frank Turner; Sarah Hudson; Richard Ashby; and finally,
Donald Greig, Reina Ruis and everyone at Jarrold.

John Curtis

Cover picture: thatched cottage at Chipping Campden

Designed and produced
by Jarrold Publishing,
Whitefriars, Norwich
NR3 1TR

All photographs
© John Curtis

Publication in this form
© Jarrold Publishing 1998,
latest reprint 2002

ISBN 0-7117-1000-7

Printed in Hong Kong.

3/02

PUBLISHER'S NOTE
Variant and archaic
spellings have been retained
in quoted material, while
the modern spellings of
place names have been used
in headings.
The inclusion of a
photograph in this book
does not necessarily imply
public access to the
building illustrated.

The Cotswolds

JOHN CURTIS

JARROLD
publishing

Roses in Calmsden

THE
COTSWOLDS

GROUNDCOVER
SERIES

Cottage garden at Wyck Rissington

Contents

N

BURIAL
MOUNDS

STANDING
STONES

HISTORIC
BUILDINGS

CHURCHES
& ABBEYS

SEVERN

A4104

M5

M50

AVON

A38

A435

A44

A44

A435

A40

GLOUCESTER

Leckhampton
Hill
(Devil's Chimney)
Crickley Hill

M5

A417

A38

A46

A419

STROUD

Rodborough
Common

Minchinhampton

Uley Tumulus

Uley Bury   Uley

A4135

North Nibley

Ozleworth

Hawkesbury
Upton

A46

Little Badminton

Great Badminton

A429

M4

PRINKNASH
ABBEY

Cranham

Painswick

Slad

Bisley

Chalford

Coberley

Birdlip
Hill

Miserden

Sapperton

Coates

OWLPEN MANOR

CHAVENAGE
HOUSE

A433

Beverstone

Tetbury

WESTONBIRT
ARBORETUM

Westonbirt

CHELTENHAM

Belas
Knap

A436

HailesAbbey

Stanway

Stanton

Winchcombe

Cleeve
Hill

SUDELEY
CASTLE

Kineton

Guiting Power

Naunton

Lower Slaughter

Snowshill

SNOWSHILL
MANOR

Broadway
TOWER

Broadway

Dover's Hill

Hidcote
Bartrim   HIDCOTE
MANOR

Chipping Campden

A44

A435

Bourton-
on-the-Hill

Moreton-
in-Marsh

Lower Swell

Adlestrop

Stow-on-the-Wold

Upper Slaughter

Wyck Rissington

Bourton-on-the-Water

Compton Abdale

Yanworth

Chedworth

Calmsden

Duntisbourne Rouse

Winson

Ablington

Bibury

Barnsley

Ampney
Crucis

CIRENCESTER

A419

CHURN

A417

A361

A420

A429

M4

Northleach

Sherborne

Little
Barrington

A40

A424

A429

LEACH

Eastleach Martin

Eastleach
Turville

Fairford

Lechlade

A361

Burford

Swinbrook

Widford Church

Minster Lovell

Filkins

Little Farringdon

A417

THAMES

A3102

White Horse
Hill

Vale of White Horse

A420

A415

WINDRUSH

Witney

A40

OXFORD

A34

A4

A415

Chastleton

Great Tew

Chipping Norton

ROLLRIGHT
STONES

A3400

A361

A4260

CHERWELL

M40

DORN

A44

A4095

EVENLODE

A424

A40

Woodstock

BLENHEIM PALACE

A417

Introduction

The Cotswolds are quintessentially English. Everything here is on a human scale, including the landscape itself where nothing exceeds Cleeve Cloud's modest 1,084 feet. I know of nowhere else in England where landscape and architecture harmonise so perfectly. Cottages, farms, manor-houses, churches, all built from the local oolitic limestone, have literally grown up out of the ground.

Many of the villages and towns are famous, and justly so. Who has not heard of Bibury, Bourton-on-the-Water, Broadway, Chipping Campden or the Slaughters? But these are the 'honey-pots'. Hidden away, often at the end of single-track lanes in deep, wooded valleys or 'bottoms', there are many more villages and hamlets, less self-conscious, less prim. Here we glimpse the secret, the real, my Cotswolds.

Returning to the Cotswolds to produce the following images proved to be both a journey of discovery and an amble down memory lane. My initial aim was to capture not only the Cotswolds of today, but also the Cotswolds I remember so vividly from my childhood. As work progressed, however, I became increasingly aware that many of the scenes would be recognisable to our forefathers of decades, even centuries ago; Ben Jonson would find Dover's Hill familiar, Alexander Pope would recognise and perhaps approve of the now-mature Cirencester Park, Henry James would still think Broadway 'delicious', and William Morris would certainly find his way around 'beautiful' Bibury. And so, as the collection of photographs grew, my anthology of the works of historians, artists, diarists, poets, travellers and the like, all of whom have been inspired or affected in some way by the Cotswolds during the last three centuries, also grew, each strangely complementing the other.

This book is a journey through the Cotswolds, starting with a look at the popular northern area around Chipping Campden and Broadway, and then progressing to the lesser-known but equally attractive southern wolds around Badminton.

Necessity meant that many of the photographs were taken 'out of season' or early or late in the day, but it is precisely at these times that we can glimpse the Cotswolds through the eyes of Jonson, Pope, James or Morris. The majority of these photographs could have been taken thirty years ago, many three centuries ago; I am confident that they will be recognisable well into the future.

John Curtis

STANTON

… Cotswold architecture. It is all accidental. An artist could never contrive it on canvas – though a mason might, if he could also paint – because so many accidents of geology, masonry, carpentry, economics, agriculture and personal temperament have combined in the production of each barn or house, each architectural group. Indeed, the whole secret of the beauties of Cotswold architecture is conveyed by the word 'unspoilt' – unspoilt by architects. Poor architects!

ROBERT HENRIQUES
The Cotswolds
1950

CHIPPING CAMPDEN

When I from Campden town depart
I leave my wits, I lose my art,
A melancholy clouds my face
I feel as though I fell from grace …

JOHN MASEFIELD
From 'Chipping Camden'
1905

CHIPPING CAMPDEN

There are no nerves or
apprehensions in the
architecture of Chipping
Campden …

SACHEVERELL SITWELL
Sacheverell Sitwell's England
1986

DOVER'S ANCIENT MEETING

23RD MAY

ON THURSDAY IN WHIT-WEEK

ON

DOVER'S HILL

near Chipping Campden, Glos.

THE SPORTS WILL COMMENCE
WITH A GOOD MATCH OF

BACKSWORDS

FOR A PURSE OF GUINEAS
TO BE PLAYED BY 9 OR 7 MEN ON A SIDE

Each side must appear in the ring by 3 o'clock in the afternoon or
15/- each pair will be given for as many as will play.

WRESTLING

FOR BELTS AND OTHER PRIZES

ALSO

JUMPING IN BAGS AND

DANCING

AND A JINGLING MATCH FOR 10/6

**AS WELL AS DIVERS OTHERS OF CELEBRATED
COTSWOLD & OLYMPICK GAMES**

OPPOSITE:
Early-nineteenth-century notice for 'Mr Robert Dover's Olympick Games upon Cotswold Hills', held on Dover's Hill near Chipping Campden.

DOVER'S HILL

The Cotswold with the
    Olympic vies
In many games and goodly
    exercise.

BEN JONSON
1636

BROADWAY TOWER

This impressive folly tower crowns Broadway Beacon and, so it is claimed, offers views of thirteen counties from its battlements. According to one story, the 6th Earl of Coventry had the tower built in 1797 when his wife expressed a desire to see whether their Cotswold estate was visible from the family seat at Croome Court, fifteen miles away near Worcester. Apparently, a bonfire was lit on the site before work commenced to confirm the fact. William Morris, Edward Burne-Jones and Rossetti stayed at the tower in the late nineteenth century.

BROADWAY

The place has so much character that it rubs off on the visitor, and if in an old garden with old gates and old walls, and old summer-houses, he lies down on the old grass it is ten to one he will be converted. It is delicious to be at Broadway …

HENRY JAMES
Article in Harper's Magazine,
New York
1889

HIDCOTE MANOR GARDEN
One of England's most influential gardens, an inspiration to both gardeners and designers.

HIDCOTE BARTRIM
Thatched cottages and farm buildings make up the hamlet beyond Hidcote Manor.

STANWAY

To all the little roads I know
Delightful haunts belong –
In hidden state lurks Stanway gate
The Stanway woods among,
The river walk between the Colnes
From Fosseway lies apart,
While Slaughter seems amid its streams
To dwell in willow-pattern dreams
Dreamt by a childish heart.

JOHN HAINES
Poems
1921

SNOWSHILL MANOR GARDEN

A garden is an extension of the house, a series of outdoor rooms. The word garden means a garth, an enclosed space. So the design was planned as a series of separate courts, sunny ones contrasting with shady ones and different courts for varying moods.

CHARLES PAGET WADE
owner of Snowshill Manor
1919–51

SNOWSHILL

From Broadway I rode along
the beautiful valley below
Middle Hill and crept up to
the retired village of
Snowshill, perched near the
summit of the ridge sloping
from the Cotswolds into the
vale, a romantic little place.
There is a good old-fashioned
mansion house ...

REV. F.E. WITTS
from a diary entry of 25 March, 1825

LITTLE BARRINGTON

A truly idyllic village with cottages perched around a large green. Depressions in the green mark the sites of quarries which provided stone, not only for the village itself, but also for rebuilding work in London following the Great Fire of 1666.

WYCK RISSINGTON

Wyck Rissington, the most northerly of the three Rissingtons (Great and Little are the others), is particularly attractive, with its wide green lined with horse chestnut trees, a duck pond and delightful stone cottages.

STOW-ON-THE-WOLD

It is a market town, situated, in
a very peculiar manner, on the
summit of a high hill ... and
exposed to every inclemency of
the weather, without the least
shelter or protection ...
It is commonly said, that *Stow
wants three elements out of the four.*

It wants water, from its high situation, and having little or no land belonging to the town, and consequently no produce of fuel, it is deficient in earth and fire; but it has air enough, which in this mountainous and exposed situation, must necessarily be very sharp and piercing, tho' pure, and perhaps, for strong constitutions, healthy.

SAMUEL RUDDER
A New History of Gloucestershire
1779

LOWER SLAUGHTER …

It has little except its loveliness … hundreds of artists … have put into pictures the little low bridges of ancient weathered stone which cross the stream flowing as clear as crystal down the street.

ARTHUR MEE
The King's England – Gloucestershire
1938

… UPPER SLAUGHTER

I thought these two villages, Lower Slaughter and Upper Slaughter, beautiful before, and think them so still. They should be preserved for ever as they are now. A man bringing a single red tile or yard of corrugated iron into these two symphonies of grey stone should be scourged out of the district.

J.B. PRIESTLEY
English Journey
1934

SWINBROOK and the RIVER WINDRUSH

The little rivers of the Cotswolds amply make up for their smallness by their beauty and variety. Clear and swift in their upper reaches ... Lower down the streams become mor placid, meandering through th narrow green meadows at the bottom of the wooded valleys and where they flow through villages crossed by little bridge of an infinite variety of design.

NORMAN JEWSON
By Chance I Did Rove
1952

WIDFOR

As interesting as it is remot the tiny church at Widfor stands on the foundations of Roman vill

BURFORD

Burford takes on the
appearance of Amsterdam
when reflected in this shop
window. Known as the
'Gateway of the Cotswolds',
it is the archetypal Cotswold
town with its main street
descending steeply to a
medieval stone four-arched
bridge crossing the
River Windrush.

SUDELEY CASTLE

Home of Katherine Parr
(who is buried in the
adjacent church), visited by
Elizabeth I, and a Royalist
headquarters during the
Civil War, Sudeley Castle
has played its part in
English history. Having
been 'slighted' in 1648, it
was partially restored
during the nineteenth
century and is today a
treasure house of priceless
art and antiques.

SHERBORNE

Mid-summer, and Cotswold gardens are ablaze with colour. Here, an apple tree shades a lovingly tended garden.

BOURTON-ON-THE-HILL

When I praised the village to the landlord of the local pub he seemed surprised, and said casually: 'Aye, it's a nice place in the spring!'

But Bourton-on-the-Hill is a nice place at any time, and on this silvery day it was exquisite. Its only street runs steeply beside a row of unpretentious but entirely lovely little cottages ...

JOHN MOORE
The Cotswolds
1937

CLEEVE HILL

'Cotswolds'

Alone I roamed the upland fields
Where Cleeve's Height meets the sky;
Alone I loved my wooded haunts
Where no strange eyes could pry.
I loved to trudge the wind-swept ridge
From Southam Wood to Fosse,
Where trailed the great grey Roman road
Long over-run with moss.
From Severn side to Cisseter
From Coombe to Birdlip Hill
I walked in simple solitude;
Unknown I lived my fill.
But things have long-since changed, they say,
And I am due to die –
Oh! would that once more I might walk
Where Cleeve's Height meets the sky.

J. C. L. MELLERSH
Poems by J. C. L. Mellersh
1933

ADLESTROP

Yes. I remember Adlestrop –
The name, because one afternoon
Of heat the express-train drew up there
Unwontedly. It was late June.

The steam hiss'd. Someone clear'd his throat.
No one left and no one came
On the bare platform. What I saw
Was Adlestrop – only the name

And willows, willow-herb, and grass,
And meadowsweet, and haycocks dry,
No whit less still and lonely fair
Than the high cloudlets in the sky.

And for that minute a blackbird sang
Close by, and round him, mistier,
Farther and farther, all the birds
Of Oxfordshire and Gloucestershire.

EDWARD THOMAS
23 June 1914

WINCHCOMBE

It is remarkable that tobacco was first planted in England in this parish, and yielded a considerable profit to the inhabitants, until they were restrained by act of parliament.

Samuel Rudder
A New History of Gloucestershire
1779

HAILES ABBEY

All that is left of Hayles is a tumble-down cloister wall with a few broken arches. It is difficult to believe that a splendid Abbey once stood here, and that pilgrims from all over England came hither over the hill from the last inn at Winchcombe to worship the precious Relic, those few drops of red fluid contained in a glass phial, 'the blode of Crist, that is in Hayles'.

JOHN MOORE
The Cotswolds
1937

NAUNTON

It is a joy to find it so small and so quiet, in the lovely wooded valley where the Windrush flows. The village is one long street of Cotswold cottages with charming gardens; the houses seem to have grown out of the hillside.

Arthur Mee
The King's England –
Gloucestershire
1938

GUITING POWER

This village … is one of those examples of how humble cottages of Cotswold stone, however simple in design, fit into the landscape and are absorbed by it.

EDITH BRILL
Portrait of the Cotswolds
1964

KINETON

… the ford at Kineton, a deep, rich, dream-like haunt, one of those which here and there on the Cotswolds give an intense, hidden delight … the hawthorn hedges meet over the stream, stone clapper bridge and road … and moorhens fuss at your approach to the water.

CHARLES & MARY HADFIELD
The Cotswolds
1966

CHASTLETON

There are country places that look as if they had stopped taking account of time a hundred years ago ... Such a place seemed Chastleton House ... that stands so imposingly beside the church, with its gables and flanking towers and façade of golden-yellow stone ... I could trespass over the fence on the opposite side of the road and go across the frosty grass to look at the big, stone pigeon-house that stands in the middle of the field.

C. HENRY WARREN
A Cotswold Year
1936

MORETON-IN-MARSH

Century after century everything here has been unhurried, quiet and orderly, and time could have been measured rather by the dial than the ticking of the clock. On the town, year after year has fallen and has left no more trace than last winter's snowflakes.

VISCOUNT SANKEY
Lord Chancellor
From a speech made at the opening of the town's new post office in 1933

THE UNDERMENTIONED TOLLS.

Will be charged in the Market Town of Moreton in Marsh on all market, fair and other days on and after this date.

Roundabouts driven by steam prohibited.

For every Roundabout driven by pony .... 5's.to 6's. per day
    ,,   Shooting Gallery. .... 5's.to 7's. 6d.
    ,,   Cocoanut Shoot. .... 2's.6d.
    ,,   Cheap John Cart. .... 2's.6d.
    ,,   Swing. . . . . . . 2's.6d. to 5's.0d.
    ,,   Waggon. . . . . . . 1's.0d.
    ,,   Cart. . . . . 6d.
    ,,   Hand Cart. . . . . . 3d.
    ,,   Stall of whatever length. . . .
        1d. per foot minimum. . . . 6d.

For Earthenware Dealers 1s. for the use of 12 sqr. yards or less and for every additional yard 1d.

For every Show, Menagerie, Bazzar, &c. not hereinbefore mentioned 1d. per square yard.

For every Caravan accompanying any of the Shows, Stalls, &c. and standing in the street 1's. per day, nothing to be allowed to stand within 18 feet of the Brick Pavement.

Residents having a stall in front of their Houses 5's. per year.

                    BY ORDER.

JOHN KENNEDY, Agent for.
THE RIGHT HON. LORD REDESDALE. K.C.V.O., C.B.
                Lord of the Manor.
                F. PAGE
                  Collector.

August 5th 1905.

BOURTON-ON-THE-WATER

This village ... is watered by a river which rises a little above it, and, as it enters the village, forms itself into an elegant serpentine canal about thirty feet wide, flowing, with an agreeable rapidity, about the depth of fourteen or fifteen inches. Many of the houses are ranged into a street, tho' somewhat irregularly, on each side of this natural canal, the banks of which being well gravelled, and very rarely overflow'd, afford a delightful walk.

SAMUEL RUDDER
A New History of Gloucestershire
1779

GREAT TEW

This must be the most quiet and contented architecture in the world.

SACHEVERELL SITWELL
Sacheverell Sitwell's England
1986

CHIPPING NORTON

The former Bliss Tweed Mill (west of the town of Chipping Norton) was built in 1872 and closed in 1980. It has since been converted into apartments.

CHIPPING NORTON

The almshouses are one of the most delightful pieces of architecture in a town rich with such rare craftsmanship.

ARTHUR MEE
The King's England – Oxfordshire
1949

WOODSTOCK

Woodstock benefits by
sitting, literally, at the gates
of Blenheim Palace. It
remains at heart a small
country town, popular for
local crafts, furniture, and
delicious cream teas.

BLENHEIM
PALACE

As we passed through
the entrance archway
and the lovely scenery
burst upon me,
Randolph said with
pardonable pride,
'This is the finest view
in England'.

LADY RANDOLPH CHURCHILL
On her first visit to Blenheim
May, 1874

ROLLRIGHT STONES   GREAT ROLLRIGHT

… what struck me most this afternoon was their splendid position up there on the bare hill-top. It was a place to catch all the sun from morning to night. Cold as the air was (there were still patches of hoar-frost in the shadows and splinters of ice in the ruts), when I touched the worn and rugged stones they were warm. I could feel the sun on my face with an intensity not usually associated with November. It was pleasant to fancy, anyway, that the place where I was standing was once a temple dedicated to the sun.

C. HENRY WARREN
A Cotswold Year
1936

WITNEY

For improvements,
'tis certain that the
Blanketing Trade of
Witney is advanced to
that height, that no
place comes near it …

Dr Plot

Professor of Chymestry,
University of Oxford
1687

MINSTER LOVELL HALL

By the River Windrush stands the ruin of Minster Lovell Hall, a fifteenth-century manor house.

BELAS KNAP
SUDELEY

The story begins at Belas Knap, the long barrow on Cleeve Cloud, the incurving horns of whose portals are the first example of the ogee shape in England. ... This ceremonial forecourt is the unacknowledged prototype of all the stone walls of field, bridge and street that are fundamental to the Cotswold scene. ... The only difference between any Cotswold stone wall and these horns of 2000 BC is that, with some exceptions, the prehistoric technique is the superior.

H. J. MASSINGHAM
Cotswold Country
1937

KEBLE BRIDGE

An old stone bridge joins the two parishes of Eastleach Martin and Eastleach Turville. It is named after the two John Kebles, father and son, who ministered to the congregations of the two medieval churches in the early nineteenth century.

ABLINGTON

One fine September evening, having left all traces of railways and the ancient Roman town of Cirencester some seven long miles behind me, with wearied limbs I sought this quiet, sequestered spot. Suddenly, as I was wondering how amid these never-ending hills there could be such a place as I had been told existed, I beheld it at my feet, surpassing beautiful! Below me was a small village, nestling amid a wealth of stately trees. The hand of man seemed in some bygone time to have done all that was necessary to render the place habitable, but no more.

J. Arthur Gibbs
A Cotswold Village
1898

FILKINS

The stone slabs serving as garden fences are a feature in this quiet village. Quarried locally, the thin 'planks' also serve as hoods over cottage doorways.

BIBURY

... surely the most beautiful village in England.

WILLIAM MORRIS
reported as said during the 1880s

LITTLE FARINGDON

A peaceful haven, the old mill at Little Faringdon is one of the last on the River Leach before it is swallowed into the Thames at nearby Lechlade.

LECHLADE

This market town of Cotswold stone stands at the highest navigable point of the Thames. Stone used in the construction of St Paul's Cathedral was loaded here.

CIRENCESTER

Cirencester remains the wealthiest town in all Cotswold. Here you will find the biggest country houses, the most expensive motors, the most beautiful hunters, the best polo ponies, the dullest society, and the most extravagant young women in Gloucestershire. It is even now as it was in Roman times; around Corinium Dobunorum rich men flourish like weeds.

JOHN MOORE
The Cotswolds
1937

CIRENCESTER

Cirencestre stondeth on Churne Ryver … Ther is now but one paroche chirch in al Cirencestre: but that is very fair. The body of the chirch is al new work … Cirencestre is in Coteswolde. Cirencestre hath the most celebrate market in al that quarters on Monday.

JOHN LELAND
Leland's Itinerary in England and Wales
In or about 1535–43

CIRENCESTER PARK

… it does not cease to be agreeable to me so late in the season; the very dying of the leaves adds a variety of colours that is not unpleasant.

ALEXANDER POPE
said in 1718
Pope assisted Allen, 1st Earl Bathurst, in laying out the park

AMPNEY CRUCIS

The head of the fifteenth-century cross was discovered walled up in the church in the mid-nineteenth century and restored to its rightful place in the churchyard. Carvings on the four faces depict the Crucifixion, the Virgin, a soldier in armour and, possibly, St Lawrence.

FAIRFORD

Fairford is a praty uplandische
toune … There is a fair mansion
place of the Tames hard by the
chirch yarde, buildid thoroughly
by John Tame and Edmunde
Tame … John Tame began the
fair new chirche of Fairforde,
and Edmund Tame finished it.

JOHN LELAND
Leland's Itinerary in England and Wales
In or about 1535–43

FAIRFORD

Fairford windows and Fairford
trout have spread abroad its
fame wherever an antiquary or
an angler is to be found.

HERBERT A. EVANS
Highways and Byways in
Oxfordshire and the Cotswolds
1905

DUNTISBOURNE LEER

Four delightful villages take their name from the Dunt brook, which rises in Duntisbourne Abbots and flows through Duntisbourne Leer, Middle Duntisbourne and Duntisbourne Rouse. The brook is forded by numerous narrow lanes, and between Duntisbourne Abbots and Duntisbourne Leer it has been diverted to follow a lane for about thirty yards to facilitate the washing of carts' wheels and horses' fetlocks.

Cottages, farms and churches are all built from the same local grey stone. In spring, walls and gardens are a mass of brightly coloured flowers. Here, cottage windows in Duntisbourne Leer are framed with wisteria and honeysuckle.

DUNTISBOURNE ROUSE

From a corner of the churchyard there is a lovely view of the stream winding through the valley, and a pretty picture of the church on a steep bank, looking like a toy church with its grey roofs going up in steps to the small old saddleback tower, every gable crowned by a cross.

ARTHUR MEE
The King's England – Gloucestershire
1938

CALMSDEN

From the top of a swell Calmsden shows a line of dormer gables on a terrace of grey houses, and deep gables of two bigger houses. Pale, grave and fresh, the village gives a geometrical appearance of lines, levels, angles and shades, without hesitations or additions. All the roofs are of an unusual light grey stone tile … the light walls of a long lane bind the village in a frame.

CHARLES & MARY HADFIELD
The Cotswolds
1967

DEVIL'S CHIMNEY
LECKHAMPTON HILL

The Devil's Chimney, a well-known landmark on the side of a precipitous cliff overlooking Cheltenham, is not a natural rock formation, as some writers would have us believe, but inferior stone left by quarrymen in the nineteenth century. The pinnacle has been consolidated, but climbing is forbidden.

CRICKLEY HILL

The Cotswold escarpment, or 'Edge', offers spectacular views, this one from Birdlip Hill looking towards Crickley Hill with its Iron Age fort and quarry workings.

BIRDLIP HILL

I looked down from the top of a high hill into the *vale of Gloucester!* Never was there, surely, such a contrast in this world! This hill is called *Burlip Hill;* it is much about a mile down it, and the descent so steep as to require the wheel of the chaise to be locked; and, even with that precaution, I did not think it over and above safe, to sit in the chaise; so upon Sir Robert Wilson's principle of taking care of *Number One,* I got out and walked down.

WILLIAM COBBETT
William Cobbett's Rural Rides
1821

COBERLEY

The River *Churn*, which passeth thro' *Cirensester* riseth in this Parish, and is there called the *Seven-Wells Head*, and the *Thames-Head*, because it is the farthest Rise of Water from the great River *Thames*, tho' there is another Spring in the Parish of *Coats* in this County, which is reputed the Head of the *Thames*, because it is the Head of the River *Isis*.

SIR ROBERT ATKYNS
The Ancient and Present
State of Glostershire
1712

CHEDWORTH

… the celebrated Roman villa at Chedworth … has been Englished by the sheer power as it seems of these exalting hills. … There could be no greater tribute to the Cotswolds than that they drew into their spell and naturalized the mentality of the most intractably foreign of all the invaders of our land.

H. J. MASSINGHAM
Cotswold Country
1937

ST ANDREW'S CHURCH

The church at Chedworth has much Norman work of the twelfth century, but it is the magnificent Perpendicular windows of the nave which impress most.

NORTHLEACH

Wool, the fine thick fleeces of the Cotswold sheep, built Northleach Church ... During the fourteenth and fifteenth centuries Northleach became the hub and centre of the whole Cotswold wool trade; and every stick and stone of Northleach owes its existence to the sheep.

JOHN MOORE
The Cotswolds
1937

When you approach St Peter and St Paul's through the churchyard from the east it looks like a great ship – the nave soaring high above the chancel ... and the tremendous tower beyond, higher still.

JOHN JULIUS NORWICH
The Architecture of Southern England
1985

CHELTENHAM

Upon the discovery of the Medicinal Spring in the beginning of the present Century, and its Efficacy being proved, and generally known, *Cheltenham* became a place of great Resort, and frequented by the best Ranks in Society. To this Circumstance it owes its present Appearance; and, as the first Cause has increased in the opinion of the Public, it has gained various Acquisitions of Improvement and Convenience. Buildings, peculiar to these Situations, of public as well as private Accomodation, have been so frequently and judiciously erected, as to make this a very respectable Specimen of a *modern* Town ...'

RALPH BIGLAND
Historical, Monumental and Genealogical Collections Relative to the County of Gloucestershire
1791

Near YANWORTH

'Men and Sheep'
The glorious churches and villages of
Cotswold were builded out of the profits of
the sheep industry

The sheep our world doth brede
  Scorn not, for they do feed
    And clothe a man in need.

And sheep may clothe a wold
  With beauties manifold
    Doubt ye? Then now behold
These churches and these towers;
  This glass which is as flowers
    Blooming despite the hours.

Ciceter, golden in peace,
  Stow, Fairford – any of these
    A cluster of heart's ease!

Ah! many a man who lies
  With face up to the skies
    Would count it Paradise,

If in his long last sleep
  A vision he could keep
    Fair as those vanished sheep;
Knowing that he had died
  For beauty, not for pride,
    For peace, and naught beside.

F.W. HARVEY
Gloucestershire
1947

COMPTON
ABDALE

Clear spring water gushes
from a curious stone
crocodile head in this
peaceful village.

WINSON

'Cotswold Ways'

One comes across the strangest things in walks:
Fragments of Abbey tithe-barns fixed in modern
And Dutch-sort houses where the water baulks
Weired up, and brick kilns broken among fern,
Old troughs, great stone cisterns bishops might have blessed
Ceremonially, and worthy mounting-stones;
Black timber in red brick, queerly placed
Where Hill stone was looked for – and a manor's bones
Spied in the frame of some wisteria'd house
And mill-falls and sedge pools and Saxon faces;
Stream-sources happened upon in unlikely places,
And Roman-looking hills of small degree
And the surprise of dignity of poplars
At a road end, or the white Cotswold scars
Or sheets spread white against the hazel tree.
Strange the large difference of up-Cotswold ways;
Birdlip climbs bold and treeless to a bend,
Portway to dim wood-lengths without end,
And Crickley goes to cliffs are the crown of days.

IVOR GURNEY   Selected Poems   1919–22

CRANHAM WOODS

Sunbeams bright as heart's desire
Bid us out and follow;
Cranham Woods are all a-fire
Over hill and hollow!

EVA DOBELL
From 'Autumn Gold'
A Bunch of Cotswold Grasses
1919

PRINKNASH ABBEY

(St Peter's Grange)
It stands on a glorious but
impracticable hill, in the midst
of a little forest of beech, and
commanding Elyseum.

HORACE WALPOLE
1774

PAINSWICK

The yews are planted in avenues; everything is very tidy and symmetrical; and although there is a popular story that the yews number ninety-nine, and that the hundredth, though often planted, has always died, I am afraid it is untrue, because there are 118. Painswick is very proud of these clipped, regimented trees; the local historian Rudder states that in his day the churchyard was 'the place of resort for the ladies and polite inhabitants of the town in fair weather'. That's the trouble; everything connected with Painswick churchyard is terribly polite and ladylike, and indeed one feels that one would have to be pretty polite before one was even allowed to be buried there.

John Moore
The Cotswolds
1937

ROCOCO GARDEN
PAINSWICK

… the garden is on an hanging ground from the house in the vale, and on a rising ground on the other side and at the end; all are cut into walks through wood and adorn'd with water and buildings, and in one part is the kitchen garden.

BISHOP POCOCKE
1757

KINGSCOTE

Arable farming has steadily increased over the centuries and today late summer weaves a rich tapestry on the wolds with fields of golden-coloured wheat, barley and oats, yellow oilseed rape, mauve linseed and white potato.

LAURIE LEE'S CHILDHOOD HOME
SLAD

I was set down from the carrier's cart at the age of three; and there with a sense of bewilderment and terror my life in the village began … That was the day we came to the village, in the summer of the last year of the First World War. To a cottage that stood in a half-acre of garden on a steep bank above a lake; a cottage with three floors and a cellar and a treasure in the walls, with a pump and apple trees, syringa and strawberries, rooks in the chimneys, frogs in the cellar, mushrooms on the ceiling, and all for three and sixpence a week.

LAURIE LEE
Cider with Rosie
1959

MISERDEN

Miserden lies at the head of the delightfully named Golden Valley. Here everything is neat and tidy and in its place. The church and churchyard are lovingly cared for, with this arch of yew standing sentinel over the approach to the south porch. The church contains Saxon work but was largely 'restored' in 1886. It is famed for its collection of carved monuments and memorials.

CHALFORD

Chalford-bottom is a deep and narrow valley about a mile in length … On the curious travellers' first approach, it presents at once a very striking and respectable appearance, consisting of a great number of well-built houses, equal to a little town, lying very contiguous, but not joined together. These are intermixt with rows of tenters, along the side of the hill, on which the cloth is stretched in the process of making. This variety of landscape is uncommonly pleasing, and so great and surprising is the acclivity where some of the buildings stand, that in different approaches to the same house, you ascend to the lowest story, and descend to the highest. In this bottom are eight fulling-mills …

SAMUEL RUDDER
A New History of Gloucestershire
1779

DRESSED WELLS
BISLEY

Well-dressing ceremonies are usually associated with Derbyshire. Here, in this remote Gloucestershire village, the seven springs which rush out of a grey stone wall in a narrow lane below the church are dressed with flowers and blessed every Ascension Day.

Near BISLEY

Bisley gates are open

(Local saying, meaning
'it is very windy')

STROUD FROM RODBOROUGH COMMON

Gloucestershire must not be passed over, without some account of a most pleasant and fruitful vale … which is called Stroud-Water; famous not for the finest cloths only, but for dying those cloths of the finest scarlets, and other grain colours that are any where in England; perhaps in any part of the world.

DANIEL DEFOE: A Tour Through The Whole Islands Of Great Britain 1724–6

SAPPERTON

The village of Sapperton has changed very little in outward appearance since I first saw it in 1907. Then there was a small cottage instead of the present house at the entrance to the village, a blacksmith's shop where the village hall now stands, and a wheelwright's yard instead of the pair of new cottages to the right of the church. These are the major changes. Minor ones are that the roads were white instead of black, there were no telegraph poles, the gardens were brighter with flowers, while in the winter there were the bright scarlet cloaks worn by the schoolchildren to add a touch of colour at a season when it was most welcome. These cloaks were the gift of Lady Bathurst.

NORMAN JEWSON
By Chance I Did Rove
1952

SAPPERTON CHURCH

Inside the church, much woodwork, including these Jacobean bench ends, came from Sapperton House, which was demolished in the 1730s.

SAPPERTON TUNNEL
COATES

Into the dim darkness you
glide and, within half an
hour, are lost in a lightless cavern
where the drip drip of the
clammy water sounds
incessantly in your ears … It was
evening when we came
out into the light again and,
though the sun had set, with
shadows falling everywhere,
it almost dazzled me.

E. TEMPLE THURSTON
The Flower of Gloster
1911

CHAVENAGE

Near Tetbury, an avenue
of beech trees leads
towards melancholy
Chavenage House, where
Cromwell once stayed.

TETBURY

Tetbury is well known for its royal associations: Highgrove
House is visible from the Parish Church and several shops display
the Royal Warrant 'by appointment' proudly. Chipping Steps
descend from one of the town's market places.

TROUBLE HOUSE INN, near TETBURY

The peaceful appearance of this inn belies a troubled past.
Two landlords, both in debt, killed themselves, and two
of England's last highwaymen were apprehended near
the inn in 1829.

BEVERSTON CASTLE

This Castle was much beautified and enlarged by the Ransom of Prisoners taken at the Battle of *Poictiers* [*sic*]. It was built square, and moated on all sides, and had a Tower at every Corner; one of the Towers is still remaining.

SIR ROBERT ATKYNS
The Ancient and Present State
of Glostershire
1712

OWLPEN

... to Owlpen I came ... Or to the end of the world, a very secret place, where a small house and a small church are screened by an abrupt, wooded conical hill at their backs and a massed guard of trained yews in front ...

H. J. Massingham
Cotswold Country
1937

VIEW FROM ULEY BURY

From the ramparts of the Iron Age fort, the view towards the River
Severn encompasses the Vale of Berkeley, Cam Peak and Dursley.

MINCHINHAMPTON COMMON BULWARKS

Did you ever hear of Enderley Flat, the highest tableland in England? Such a fresh, free, breezy spot – how the wind sweeps over it!

MRS CRAIK
John Halifax – Gentleman
1856

(when writing *John Halifax – Gentleman* in the 1850s, Mrs Craik stayed at Amberley and based Enderley Flat on nearby Minchinhampton Common)

MINCHINHAMPTON

The Town is situated upon a gradual Declevity, open to the South-east, from whence the Approach is very picturesque. It consists of four Streets, lying at right Angles, but irregularly built. A beautiful Skreen of Wood surrounds it on the North-west, in the higher Ground of the Park, which gives every distant View of the singularly shaped Tower a very pleasing Effect, as it appears 'besomed high in tufted Trees'.

RALPH BIGLAND
Historical, Monumental and Genealogical Collections Relative to the County of Gloucestershire
1791

ULEY TUMULUS

(Hetty Pegler's Tump)
Cotswold is a country richer
in chambered long barrows
even than Wiltshire, and the
Tump is one of the most
perfect in England. Thus the
Cotswold stone was
consecrated four thousand
years ago, and the spirits
of the dead were sanctified
by the act of entering into it
and dwelling there.

H. J. MASSINGHAM
Cotswold Country
1937

OZLEWORTH BOTTOM

In this part of the
Cotswolds, near
Wotton-under-Edge,
the deep secret
valleys are commonly
known as 'Bottoms'.
Ozleworth Bottom
is heavy with the
smell of wild garlic
in springtime.

SOMERSET MONUMENT
HAWKESBURY UPTON

Standing north of the village, this monument recalls Lord Robert Edward Henry Somerset, a member of the Beaufort family, who served with distinction at the Battle of Waterloo.

WESTONBIRT ARBORETUM

Westonbirt was begun in 1829. Since then it has become one of England's finest arboreta, with more than 4,000 different trees and shrubs. It is especially spectacular in the autumn, when the variety of colour is stunning.

TYNDALE MONUMENT
NORTH NIBLEY

[William Tyndale's] work remains, and is likely long to remain, loved and reverenced by all English-speaking people throughout the world, as their noblest inheritance; but the man, to whose patient labour and heroic self-sacrifice we are mainly indebted for the English Bible, has been allowed to almost drop out of memory.

REV. R. DEMAUS M.A.
William Tyndale – A Biography
1871

Near HILLSLEY

From a country lane, a glimpse through a gate reveals a secret countryside.

GREAT BADMINTON

Badminton [House] has always been the grandest seat in Gloucestershire. With its vast estates, it is still a sort of principality, still with a reigning duke. Yet there is an unaccountable homeliness about it. It is approached through the pretty village with its colour-washed cottages, past some rather unducal gates, down a short drive leading to an outer court where the cars are washed, under a stable arch, through another open courtyard with a *porte cochère* on one side and a duckpond on the other, under an impressive William Kent pavilion, and into the forecourt. This route suggests having crossed a frontier, of having entered a Ruritanian kingdom whose capital is the village and palace the house. And what a palace! ... the hall is one of the noblest state-rooms in the Cotswolds. It was here during a particularly inclement winter in 1863 that the children of the 8th Duke invented the game of Badminton.

JAMES LEES-MILNE
Some Cotswold Country Houses
1987

LITTLE BADMINTON

In the Cotswolds ... the visual
pleasures belong to the valleys,
and even there the scenery
plays second fiddle to the
architecture ... it is the villages
and farms which charm us most
... it is the buildings that steal
the picture.

ALEC CLIFTON-TAYLOR
Another Six English Towns
1984

Bibliography

Atkyns, Sir Robert: *The Ancient and Present State of Glostershire.* First published 1712; republished by E.P. Publishing Ltd in collaboration with Gloucestershire County Library, 1974.

Beckinsale, R.P: *Companion ino Gloucestershire,* Methuen, 1939. [source of poster on p.16.]

Bigland, Ralph: *Historical, Monumental and Genealogical Collections Relative to the County of Gloucestershire.* Bristol & Gloucestershire Archaeological Society, 1989.

Brill, Edith: *Portrait of the Cotswolds,* Robert Hale Ltd, 1964.

Churchill, Lady Randolph: *The Reminiscences of Lady Randolph Churchill,* 1908

Clifton-Taylor, Alec: *Another Six English Towns.* BBC, 1984.

Cobbett, William: *William Cobbett's Illustrated Rural Rides 1821–1832.* Webb & Bower, 1984.

Mrs Craik: *John Halifax – Gentleman.* J.M. Dent, 1961.

Defoe, Daniel: *A Tour Through The Whole Islands Of Great Britain, 1724–6.* Penguin, 1971

Demaus, Rev. R: *William Tyndale – A Biography.* The Religious Tract Society, London, 1886.

Dobell, Eva: *A Bunch of Cotswold Grasses.* A.H. Stockwell, London, 1919.

Evans, Herbert A: *Highways and Byways in Oxfordshire and the Cotswolds.* Macmillan & Co Ltd, London, 1905.

Gibbs, J. Arthur: *A Cotswold Village.* John Murray, London, 1898.

Gurney, Ivor: *Collected Poems of Ivor Gurney,* edited by P.J. Kavanagh. Oxford University Press, 1982.

Hadfield, Charles and Mary: *The Cotswolds.* B.T. Batsford, 1966.

Haines, John: *Poems.* Selwyn & Blount Ltd, London, 1921.

Harvey, F.W: *Gloucestershire: A selection of poems by F.W. Harvey.* Oliver & Boyd, Edinburgh and London, 1947.

Henriques, Robert: *The Cotswolds.* Paul Elek Publishers Ltd, 1950.

James, Henry: *see* Verey, David

Jewson, Norman: *By Chance I Did Rove.* Earle & Ludlow, 1952; republished privately by Norman Jewson 1973.

Lee, Laurie: *Cider with Rosie.* The Hogarth Press, 1959.

Lees-Milne, James: *Some Cotswold Country Houses.* The Dovecote Press Ltd, 1987.

— *Earls of Creation.* Hamish Hamilton Ltd, 1962. [source of Alexander Pope quotation on p. 65.]

Leland, John: *Leland's Itinerary in England and Wales.* Southern Illinois University Press, 1964.

Masefield, John: 'Chipping Campden' (poem), The Society of Authors, 1905

Massingham, H.J: *Cotswold Country.* B.T. Batsford Ltd, 1937.

McCarthy, Fiona: *William Morris – A Life For Our Time.* Faber & Faber, 1994.

Mee, Arthur: *The King's England – Gloucestershire.* Hodder & Stoughton, 1938; revised edition 1966.

— *The King's England – Oxfordshire.* Hodder & Stoughton, 1949; revised edition 1965.

Mellersh, J.C.L: *Poems.* Oxford University Press, 1933.

Moore, John: *The Cotswolds.* Ebenezer Baylis & Sons Ltd, 1837.

Morris, William: *see* McCarthy, Fiona

Norwich, John Julius: *The Architecture of Southern England.* Macmillan, 1985.

Plot, Dr: quoted in *Ward Lock's The Cotswolds.* Ward, Lock and Co Ltd, 1949.

Pope, Alexander: *see* Lees-Milne, James.

Priestley, J.B: *English Journey.* Reed Books (William Heinemann), 1934.

Rudder, Samuel: *A New History of Gloucestershire.* First published 1779; republished by Sutton Publishing Ltd in collaboration with Gloucestershire County Library.

Sankey, Viscount: quoted in *The North Cotswolds in Old Photographs,* collected by David Viner. Sutton Publishing Ltd, 1988.

Sitwell, Sacheverell: *Sacheverell Sitwell's England,* edited by Michael Raeburn. Little, Brown (Orbis), 1986.

Thomas, Edward: 'Adlestrop'(poem). Oxford University Press, 1914.

Thurston, E. Temple: *The Flower of Gloster.* Williams & Norgate, London, 1911.

Verey, David: *The Shell Book of English Villages.* Michael Joseph, 1980. [source of Henry James quotation on p. 18.]

— (ed.) *Diary of a Cotswold Parson* (Rev. F.E Witts). Sutton Publishing Ltd, 1978. [source of Horace Walpole quotation on p. 88.]

Wade, Charles Paget: quoted in *Days Far Away,* The National Trust, 1996.

Walpole, Horace: *see* Verey, David.

Warren, C. Henry. *A Cotswold Year.* Geoffrey Bles, 1936; republished by Sutton Publishing Ltd, 1985.

Witts, Rev. F.E: *see* Verey, David.

Acknowledgements

Every effort has been made to secure permission from copyright owners to use the extracts of text featured in this book. Any subsequent correspondence should be sent to Jarrold Publishing at the address given at the start.

page

13 from *The Cotswolds* by Robert Henriques. Paul Elek Publishers Ltd, 1950.

14 (left) *'Chipping Campden'* by John Masefield (written in 1905), by kind permission of the Society of Authors as the Literary Representative of the the Estate of John Masefield.

14 (right) from *Sacheverell Sitwell's England* by Sacheverell Sitwell, edited by Michael Raeburn. Little, Brown & Co. (Orbis), 1986. By courtesy of the publishers.

16 Poster quoted in *Companion into Gloucestershire* by R.P. Beckinsale, Methuen, 1939.

18 (right) From an article by Henry James entitled *'Our Artists in Europe'* in Harper's Magazine, New York, 1889.

Quoted in *The Shell Book of English Villages*. Michael Joseph, 1980.

21 From *Poems by John Haines*. Selwyn & Blount Ltd, London, 1921.

22 Charles Paget Wade quoted in *Days Far Away*, The National Trust, 1996.

23 From *The Diary of a Cotswold Parson – Reverend F.E. Witts 1783–1854*, edited by David Verey. Sutton Publishing Ltd, 1978. [Diary extracts © 1978 Francis Witts.]

27 From *A New History of Gloucestershire* by Samuel Rudder. First published 1779, republished by Sutton Publishing Ltd in collaboration with Gloucestershire County Library.

28 (left) From *The King's England – Gloucestershire* by Arthur Mee. Hodder & Stoughton 1938; revised edition 1966.

28 (right) From *English Journey* by J.B. Priestley. Reed Books (William Heinemann), 1934. By courtesy of the publishers.

30 From *By Chance I Did Rove* by Norman Jewson. Earle & Ludlow 1952; republished privately by Norman Jewson 1973. © 1973 Norman Jewson

35 From *The Cotswolds* by John Moore. Ebenezer Baylis & Sons Ltd, 1937.

37 (left) Poem first published in *'The Salopian'*, 13 June 1931. Taken from *Poems by J.C.L. Mellersh*. Oxford University Press, 1933. By courtesy of Blackwell Publishers.

39 From *A New History of Gloucestershire* by Samuel Rudder. First published 1779, republished by Sutton Publishing Ltd in collaboration with Gloucestershire County Library.

40 From *The Cotswolds* by John Moore. Ebenezer Baylis & Sons Ltd, 1937.

41 From *The King's England – Gloucestershire* by Arthur Mee. Hodder & Stoughton 1938; revised edition 1966.

43 (left) From *Portrait of the Cotswolds* by Edith Brill. Robert Hale Ltd, 1964. By courtesy of the publishers.

43 (right) From *The Cotswolds* by Charles and Mary Hadfield. B.T. Batsford Ltd, 1966. Quoted by kind permission of B.T. Batsford Ltd.

44 (left) From *A Cotswold Year* by C. Henry Warren. First published 1936 by Geoffrey Bles; republished 1985 by Sutton Publishing Ltd. © Estate of C. Henry Warren 1936, 1985.

44 (right) From a speech made by Viscount Sankey in 1933, quoted in *The North Cotswolds in Old Photographs*,

collected by David Viner. Sutton Publishing Ltd, 1988.

47 (left) From *A New History of Gloucestershire* by Samuel Rudder. First published 1779, republished by Sutton Publishing Ltd in collaboration with Gloucestershire County Library.

47 (right) from *Sacheverell Sitwell's England* by Sacheverell Sitwell, edited by Michael Raeburn. Little, Brown & Co. (Orbis), 1986. By courtesy of the publishers.

49 From *The King's England – Oxfordshire* by Arthur Mee. Hodder & Stoughton, 1949; revised edition 1965.

52 From *A Cotswold Year* by C. Henry Warren. First published 1936 by Geoffrey Bles; republished 1985 by Sutton Publishing Ltd. © Estate of C. Henry Warren 1936, 1985.

53 From *Natural History of Oxfordshire* by Dr Plot (1687), quoted in *Ward Lock's The Cotswolds*. Ward, Lock and Co. Ltd, 1949).

54 (right) From *Cotswold Country* by H.J. Massingham. B.T. Batsford Ltd, 1937. Quoted by kind permission of B.T. Batsford Ltd.

58 (right) William Morris quoted in *William Morris – A Life For Our Time* by Fiona McCarthy. Faber & Faber,

Wolds near Daglingworth

1994. By courtesy of the publishers.

62 (left) From *The Cotswolds* by John Moore. Ebenezer Baylis & Sons Ltd, 1937.

62 (right) From *Leland's Itinerary in England and Wales* by John Leland. First published circa 1535–43, republished 1964 by Southern Illinois University Press.

65 (left) From a letter written by Alexander Pope to the Blount sisters on 8th Oct 1718. Quoted in *Earls of Creation* by James Lees-Milne. Hamish Hamilton Ltd, 1962.

66 From *Leland's Itinerary in England and Wales* by John Leland. First published circa 1535–43, republished 1964 by Southern Illinois University Press.

67 From *Highways and Byways in Oxfordshire and the Cotswolds* by Herbert A. Evans. Macmillan & Co Ltd, London, 1905.

70 From *The King's England – Gloucestershire* by Arthur Mee. Hodder & Stoughton 1938; revised edition 1966.

73 From *The Cotswolds* by Charles and Mary Hadfield. B.T. Batsford Ltd, 1966. Quoted by kind permission of B.T. Batsford Ltd.

76 From *William Cobbett's Illustrated Rural Rides* (1821–1832) by William Cobbett, republished by Webb & Bower, 1984.

77 From *The Ancient and Present State of Glostershire* by Sir Robert Atkyns. First published 1712, republished 1974 by E.P. Publishing Ltd in collaboration with Gloucestershire County Library.

78 (top) From *Cotswold Country* by H.J. Massingham. B.T. Batsford Ltd, 1937. Quoted by kind permission of B.T. Batsford Ltd.

81 (top) From *The Cotswolds* by John Moore. Ebenezer Baylis & Sons Ltd, 1937.

81 (bottom) From *The Architecture of Southern England* by John Julius Norwich. Macmillan, 1985. By courtesy of the publishers.

83 From *Historical, Monumental and Genealogical Collections Relative to the County of Gloucestershire* by Ralph Bigland. First published 1791, republished 1989 by the Bristol & Gloucestershire Archaeological Society.

85 From *Gloucestershire*, a selection of poems by F.W. Harvey. Oliver & Boyd, Edinburgh and London, 1947. Copyright use permission: Patrick Harvey.

87 Reprinted from *The Collected Poems of Ivor Gurney*, edited by P.J. Kavanagh, 1982. By permission of Oxford University Press.

88 (left) From *A Bunch of Cotswold Grasses* by Eva Dobell. A.H. Stockwell, London, 1919.

88 (right) Quoted in the footnotes of *The Diary of a Cotswold Parson – Reverend F.E. Witts 1783–1854*, edited by David Verey (notes © David Verey 1978). Sutton Publishing Ltd, 1978.

91 From *The Cotswolds* by John Moore. Ebenezer Baylis & Sons Ltd, 1937.

95 (left) From *Cider with Rosie* by Laurie Lee. The Hogarth Press, 1959. By courtesy of Random House UK Ltd (The Hogarth Press).

97 (left) From *A New History of Gloucestershire* by Samuel Rudder. First published 1779, republished by Sutton Publishing Ltd in collaboration with Gloucestershire County Library.

100 From *By Chance I Did Rove* by Norman Jewson. Earle & Ludlow 1952; republished privately by Norman Jewson 1973. © 1973 Norman Jewson

102 (left) From *The Flower of Gloster* by E. Temple Thurston. Williams & Norgate, London, 1911.

106 From *The Ancient and Present State of Glostershire* by Sir Robert Atkyns. First published 1712, republished 1974 by E.P. Publishing Ltd in collaboration with Gloucestershire County Library.

108 From *Cotswold Country* by H.J. Massingham. B.T. Batsford Ltd, 1937. Quoted by kind permission of B.T. Batsford Ltd.

111 (left) From *John Halifax – Gentleman* by Mrs Craik. First published 1856, republished by J. M. Dent 1961.

111 (right) From *Historical, Monumental and Genealogical Collections Relative to the County of Gloucestershire* by Ralph Bigland. First published 1791, republished 1989 by the Bristol & Gloucestershire Archaeological Society.

112 (left) From *Cotswold Country* by H.J. Massingham. B.T. Batsford Ltd, 1937. Quoted by kind permission of B.T. Batsford Ltd.

117 (left) From *William Tyndale – A Biography* by the Reverend R. Demaus M.A. First published 1871; new edition revised by Richard Lovett M.A. published by the Religious Tract Society, London, 1886.

118 From *Some Cotswold Country Houses* by James Lees-Milne. The Dovecote Press Ltd, 1987. By courtesy of the publishers.

120 From *Another Six English Towns* by Alec Clifton-Taylor. BBC, 1984. Reproduced with the permission of BBC Worldwide Limited.

The Market Hall at Tetbury

Index

GROUNDCOVER
SERIES